MONKEYS

Sophie Davies and Diana Bentley

Illustrated by Karen Johnson

Key to illustrations

MONKEYS

Sophie Davies and Diana Bentley

Illustrated by

Karen Johnson

PUFFIN BOOKS

Monkeys live in hot places like Africa, Asia and South America.

Some monkeys live up in the trees in big forests. Other monkeys live down on the ground in the daytime, but at night they go to sleep up in the trees.

Did you know that monkeys can be red, brown, black, grey or black and white?

Spider monkeys have long, thin arms
and legs so they look a bit like spiders.
Some monkeys have very long noses.

Monkeys need long arms and legs to help them leap, run and climb.

Most monkeys have long tails. Some
monkeys can use their tails to hold on
to branches.

Monkeys usually eat leaves, grass and fruit, but some monkeys eat insects, birds' eggs, frogs and lizards as well.

The mother monkey usually has one baby at a time. When it is small, the baby hangs on to the fur on her belly.

When the baby is bigger, it rides on its mother's back. Later it learns to swing through the trees.

Many monkeys are in danger. People are cutting down the forests where they live. We must save the forests if we want to save these monkeys.